The Skeleton Inside You

by Philip Balestrino
illustrated by True Kelley

Revised Edition

HarperCollins*Publishers*

For my mother, Lillian Balestrino,
and for Fred Haynes   —P.B.

For the children of Warner, New Hampshire
—T.K.

Other Recent Let's-Read-and-Find-Out Science Books® You Will Enjoy

How We Learned the Earth Is Round • My Feet • My Hands • An Octopus Is Amazing • What Will the Weather Be? • Ears Are For Hearing • Earthquakes • Fossils Tell of Long Ago • My Five Senses • What Happened to the Dinosaurs? • Shooting Stars • A Drop of Blood • Switch On, Switch Off • The Skeleton Inside You • Feel the Wind • Ducks Don't Get Wet • Tornado Alert • Digging Up Dinosaurs • The Beginning of the Earth • Eclipse • The Sun: Our Nearest Star • Dinosaur Bones • Glaciers • Snakes Are Hunters • Danger—Icebergs! • Comets • Evolution • Rockets and Satellites • The Planets in Our Solar System • The Moon Seems to Change • Ant Cities • Get Ready for Robots! • Gravity Is a Mystery • Snow Is Falling • Journey into a Black Hole • What Makes Day and Night • Air Is All Around You • Turtle Talk • What the Moon Is Like • Hurricane Watch • Sunshine Makes the Seasons • My Visit to the Dinosaurs • The BASIC Book • Bits and Bytes • Germs Make Me Sick! • Flash, Crash, Rumble, and Roll • Volcanoes • Dinosaurs Are Different • What Happens to a Hamburger • Meet the Computer • How to Talk to Your Computer • Rock Collecting • Is There Life in Outer Space? • All Kinds of Feet • Flying Giants of Long Ago • Rain and Hail • Why I Cough, Sneeze, Shiver, Hiccup, & Yawn • The Sky Is Full of Stars

The *Let's-Read-and-Find-Out Science Book* series was originated by Dr. Franklyn M. Branley, Astronomer Emeritus and former Chairman of the American Museum–Hayden Planetarium, and was formerly co-edited by him and Dr. Roma Gans, Professor Emeritus of Childhood Education, Teachers College, Columbia University. For a complete catalog of Let's-Read-and-Find-Out Science Books, write to HarperCollins Children's Books, a division of HarperCollins Publishers, 10 East 53rd Street, New York, N.Y. 10022.

Library of Congress Cataloging-in-Publication Data
Balestrino, Philip.
    The Skeleton inside you / by Philip Balestrino ; illustrated by True Kelley.—Rev. ed.
        p.   cm. — (A Let's-read-and-find-out science book)

    Summary: An introduction to the human skeletal system, explaining how the 206 bones of the skeleton join together, how they grow, how they help make blood, what happens when they break, and how they mend.
    1. Human skeleton—juvenile literature.   [1. Skeleton.
2. Bones.]   I. Kelley, True, ill.   II. Title.   III. Series.
QM101.B35   1989   88-23672
611—dc19   CIP
ISBN 0-690-04731-2   AC
ISBN 0-690-04733-9 (lib. bdg.)
"A Harper Trophy book"
(A Let's-read-and-find-out book)
ISBN 0-06-445087-2 (pbk.)   88-24600

The Skeleton Inside You

On Halloween I wore a skeleton costume. I used to think skeletons were made up just to scare people. Now I know that skeletons are real. They are not scary. I would not be me without a skeleton. You would not be you.

Skeletons are made up of many bones. Bones give you shape. A ball of clay has no bones inside it. You can make a ball of soft clay into any shape you want. You can make it into a little figure. Then you can squash the figure and roll it into a mustache or a snake. But nothing can change your shape, because you have a skeleton inside you.

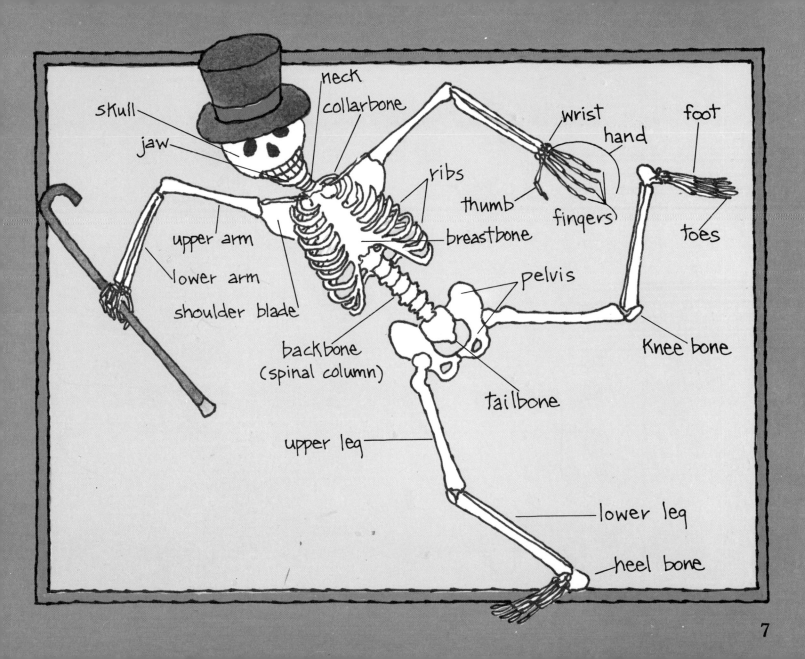

skull

jaw

neck

collarbone

wrist

hand

foot

thumb

fingers

toes

ribs

breastbone

upper arm

lower arm

shoulder blade

pelvis

Knee bone

backbone
(spinal column)

tailbone

upper leg

lower leg

heel bone

7

A marionette has a skeleton too, but it is made of
wood and wire, not of real bones.

A plain wooden chair is like a skeleton without any covering. When the chair is covered with stuffing and cloth, it is like your skeleton covered with muscles and skin. But your skeleton is different. It is made up of bones.

Your skeleton is made up of 206 bones. There are 64 bones just in your two hands and arms. Some of your bones are big, others are small. Some bones are flat, others are round.

Bones are hard. They give your body shape. Your ears and nose have something called cartilage in them to give them shape. Cartilage is softer than bone, and so it can bend. When the barber folds over your ear to cut your hair, your ear does not break off. That's because of the soft cartilage in your ear.

Once I pushed my nose flat against a bakery window to look at some cookies. My nose didn't hurt, and it didn't break off. It came back to the same shape. Push your nose flat. It will bend too, because it has cartilage inside it.

Sometimes bones get broken. I fell out of a tree once and broke my arm. My mother took me to the doctor. The doctor took an X ray. Then he fitted the bone back together. Next the doctor put a stiff plaster cast on my arm to keep the bone together. I had a sling around my neck to hold my arm and the plaster cast. For several weeks I wore the cast. All the time, the bone was growing back together. When the doctor took off the plaster cast, my bone was all healed.

Bones live and grow, just like every other part of the body. Bones start to grow before you are even born. As your bones grow longer, you grow taller, until you're all grown.

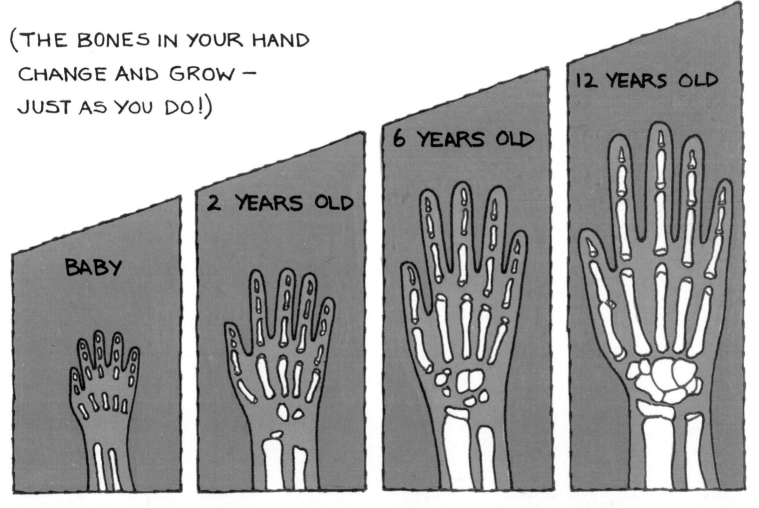

(THE BONES IN YOUR HAND
CHANGE AND GROW —
JUST AS YOU DO!)

BABY

2 YEARS OLD

6 YEARS OLD

12 YEARS OLD

Foods like milk and cheese and some leafy vegetables have calcium in them. Calcium is a mineral that helps bones grow. Calcium also makes bones hard. Without it, all your bones would be as soft as cartilage. They would be soft enough to tie into knots.

The butcher cut up a big soup bone for my mother. The inside of it looked like this:

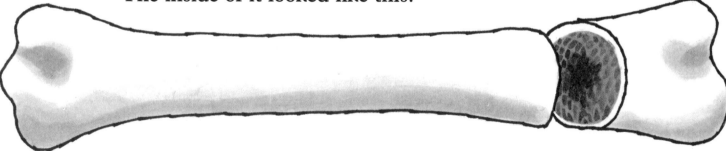

It was a bone from a big steer's leg. Your leg bones look almost the same inside.

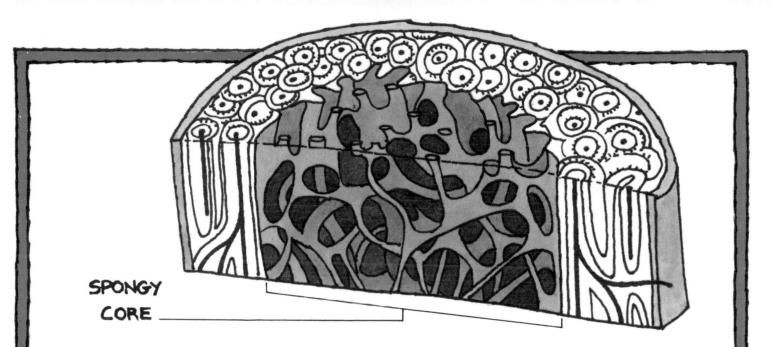

SPONGY
CORE

Inside your bones is a core that looks something like a sponge. All the little spaces in the core are filled with soft bone marrow. Bone marrow helps make the red cells of your blood.

The insides of bones store calcium and other minerals that come from the food you eat. These minerals are saved up until your body needs them.

All your 206 bones fit together to make your skeleton.
Your skeleton helps you stand up straight.

Without a skeleton, you would be like a ball of soft clay that can be molded into anything. You would be as floppy as a big beanbag.

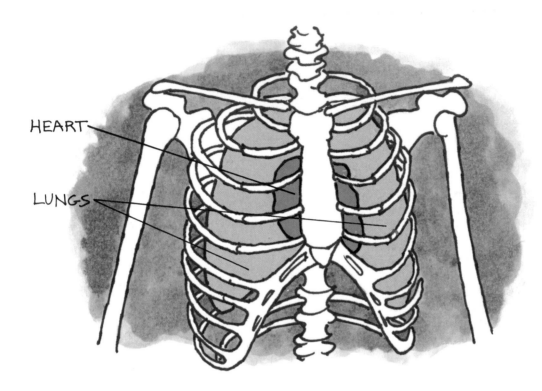

HEART

LUNGS

Some bones in your skeleton protect important parts inside you. Your rib bones cover your heart and lungs. Your skull protects your brain from hard knocks. The bones around your eyes protect them the way a football helmet does.

Your skeleton also helps you walk, run, and jump and move in many ways.

The bones of your skeleton fit together at joints.
Without joints, your skeleton could not move or bend.
Shoulders, elbows, and ankles are joints.

SHOULDER JOINT

ELBOW JOINT

ANKLE JOINT

27

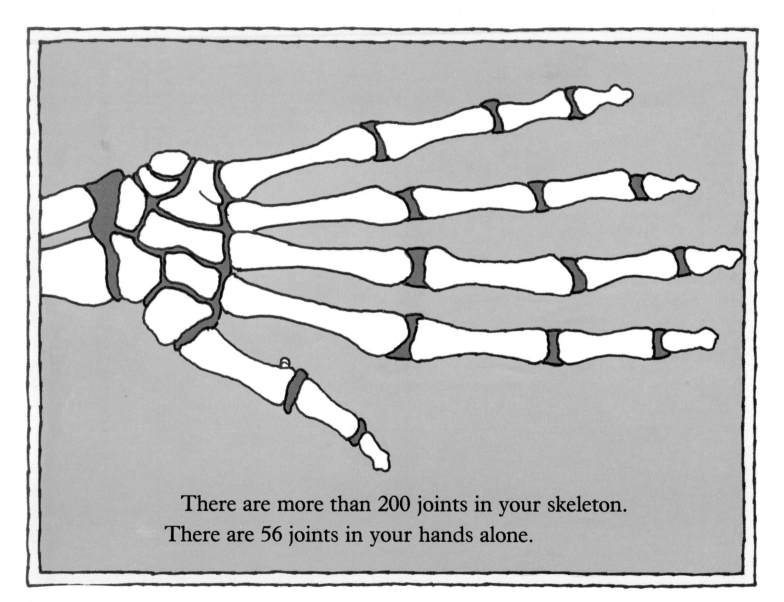

There are more than 200 joints in your skeleton.
There are 56 joints in your hands alone.

The bones are held at the joints by ligaments. Ligaments are like strong pieces of string. They hold the bones together at the joints. But they also slide back and forth and sideways to let the bones move.

KNEE JOINT

KNEE

LIGAMENTS

Your backbone is made up of 34 bones that fit together at 33 separate joints. That is why you can twist and turn almost any way. You can do a somersault. Or you can make yourself into a bridge, back up or belly up. If a backbone were only one bone, you could not do these things.

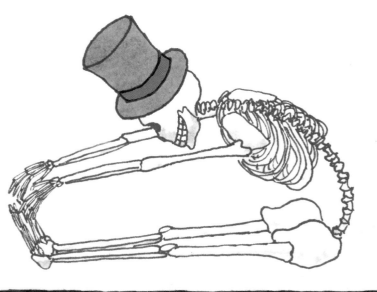

You could not put on a scary skeleton suit. You would not be able to run or jump or ring doorbells on Halloween if you did not have a skeleton inside you.